Susanna Watts (1768 to 1842)

Author of Leicester's First Guide, Abolitionist and Bluestocking

For Joan

Best Wishes

Shirley Aucott

Shirley Aucott

First published in 2004

ISBN 0-9548189-0-3

Design layout by Shirley Aucott and Angela Chorley.

Printed by Audio Visual Services, University of Leicester, Leicester.

Published by Shirley Aucott.

Front cover picture -
*A self-portrait of Susanna Watts, drawn circa 1834. Copyright held by the
Record Office of Leicester, Leicestershire and Rutland.*

Back cover picture-
*Danetts Hall, painted from West Bridge (circa 1800) by Miss Payne. Copyright
held by Leicester City Museums Service.*

All other pictures -
Copyright held by the Record Office of Leicester, Leicestershire and Rutland.

Acknowledgements

This biography of Susanna Watts has developed out of the presently unpublished writing of another book, which covers the lives of one hundred women, who have been either born, or lived for some time, in Leicester. Aspects of Susanna's life are included in this larger book, but because so little has actually been written about her life and because 2004 is the bicentenary of her famous publication, *A Walk Through Leicester,* it seems appropriate to mark the occasion with a more detailed biography. Many people have shown a great deal of interest in the writing of both books and due acknowledgement will be given to them when the larger book is published. For the people who have shown enthusiasm and given their encouragement for this book I give my sincere thanks. For help with the research I would particularly like to extend my thanks to all of the staff at the Record Office of Leicester, Leicestershire and Rutland. They have shown a genuine interest in my research, fetched me countless documents from the strong room, deciphered unclear words, given advice and made various suggestions. Julia Collieu, Curator of Fine Art, at New Walk Museum and Art Gallery, has been very patient and helpful concerning a particular picture in this publication. Aubrey Stevenson, Alan McWhirr and Ian Proctor-Blain have provided me with invaluable information concerning publishing, for which I am very grateful. Angela Chorley, Manager of the Audio Visual Services Department at the University of Leicester, has been kind, supportive and encouraging. She has given me immeasurable help and guidance with the publication of this book and I remain indebted to her. Colin Hyde has also given some very welcome instruction with regard to the use of computer software. My final thanks go to my husband, John, for giving me the time and the space to write. His support, patience and encouragement has, and continues to be, unstinting.

Contents

1802 Map of Leicester, used by Susanna in her guide

Introduction

Susanna Watts is best known as the woman who wrote the first guide to Leicester, *A Walk through Leicester: being A Guide to Strangers, containing A Description of the Town and It's Environs, with remarks upon its History and Antiquities.* This very fine volume was first published, anonymously, in 1804. It is, therefore, very apt that this biography should be published during the bicentenary year of the guide's publication. A second edition, with some additional information, appeared in 1821, and a re-print of the first edition, in 1902. Because of the guide's intrinsic value to our understanding of Leicester and its environs in the early part of the nineteenth century, and because it was one of the earliest guide books ever written in England, Leicester University Press published a facsimile reprint, with an introduction by Professor Jack Simmons, in 1967. In this he claims that the only other large industrial cities which can lay claim to having had guides written before Susanna's are Newcastle, Bristol and Liverpool

Apart from being the author of *A Walk through Leicester*, little else is known about Susanna's life and reputation. There was a small memoir written about her life, and posthumously published, in *The Fragment Gatherer,* which was sold in aid of the Baptist Mission. This was then extended and reprinted under the title *Hymns and Poems of the Late Susanna Watts with a few Recollections of her Life.* The author of this publication was unknown, but it was thought to have been a former pupil of hers. The information in this very slender text was, in turn, used by Samuel Coltman when writing his memoirs of the Coltman family in *Times Stepping Stones: Memorials of Four Generations of a Family – By a Member of the Same.*

Apart from the above rather short biographical sketches and fragments of information in local history texts, some of which are incorrect and misleading, there seems to have been nothing of any real substance written about Susanna's life and work. Although there are few personal records that have survived from which to write anything of great length, the material that has survived is certainly sufficient to warrant the writing of this biography. One of the main, invaluable sources that I have used has been Susanna's own scrapbook. This is somewhat of a 'rag bag' of poems, letters, drawings, translations, hymns, prayers, pictures, extracts of sermons, newspaper cuttings and various ephemera selected and collected by Susanna throughout her life. For example, one of the more light-hearted items which Susanna chose to paste into her scrapbook in

1834 was a handbill advertising 'The extraordinary Exhibition of The Industrious Fleas'. This was held at Mr Gee's, who was a boot maker in Leicester's market place. The handbill promised to show, at the cost of one shilling for adults and sixpence for children less than ten years of age:

> A first-rate man-of-war [with] 120 guns, sails, rigging, anchors and everything requisite in a real Three-Decker, not forgetting a numerous crew, which placed on a Gold Car with four wheels, is Drawn by a Single Flea.

Examples such as this in Susanna's scrapbook have provided some amazing insights into the many and varied aspects of her life, whilst at the same time acting as a vehicle and guide to other sources that contain primary and secondary evidence.

Some time shortly before her death, in February 1842, Susanna gave the scrapbook, for safe keeping, to her long and trusted friend, Mary Ann Coltman. She, in her turn, then gave it to her great, great niece, Clara Parkes. From her it seems to have been passed to another relative, by the name of Miss J D Parkes, who gave it to Leicester Municipal Library in October 1937. It is now safely lodged with the Record Office of Leicester, Leicestershire and Rutland.

If it is only for the fact that Susanna bequeathed to us her incredible guide to Leicester, which can still be used and enjoyed today, then I believe she deserves some form of recognition for having written and published it. This is one of the reasons why this biography has been written, but there are several other aspects of her life that I also believe need to be recognised, recorded and celebrated. They include what must surely have been the greatest work of her life, her total dedication to the abolitionist cause. In addition, her commitment to relieving the poverty and degradation of the elderly of Leicester, through her establishment of the Society for Indigent Old Age, deserves recognition. A great deal of her work and success resulted from the fact that she was a strong-minded and principled woman, with a highly developed social conscience, a great deal of determination and forceful Bluestocking sentiments.

Susanna's social conscience and forceful personality often manifests itself in her poems. They give an invaluable insight into her beliefs, interests and activities throughout most of her life, for through the medium of poetry Susanna was very adept at expressing her opinions and emotions. Because of her clear love of poetry and her lifelong ability to express herself through poetic form, I have woven many examples into this biography. Some poems mark particular events and celebrations, from the simple to the sublime, while others express strong opinions and forceful responses to criticism.

Susanna Watts – A Life

There is only one known surviving image of Susanna and that is a self-drawn portrait in her scrapbook. There may well be another image that has survived somewhere within her remaining family, for in her will she bequeaths to her cousin, William Mosley Watts, the Watts family pictures and seals. The self-drawn portrait of Susanna reveals a rather slight figure and this is confirmed, and her character elaborated on by Samuel Coltman, in *Times Stepping Stones:*

[She was] very delicate in form and complexion – like a sylph in her movements – with fair hair and feminine softness of countenance – Every way lovely, gentle, retiring and most patient. . .[1]

Another description of her appearance is given in a letter written by the novelist, Maria Edgeworth, in 1802 'Miss Watts, a tall young lady in white, fresh colour, fair thin oval face, rather pretty.'[2]

Susanna was the youngest daughter of John and Joan Watts of Danetts Hall. The Hall was situated on what is now King Richard's Way. It was purchased and rebuilt by Susanna's great grandfather, John Watts, some time in the early eighteenth century. Upon his death, in 1742, William Watts, his grandson, succeeded to the Hall, his father, John, having died in December 1726 and his mother, Elizabeth (nee Moseley), in August 1728. William, according to Nichols, did not remain the owner of the Hall, but sold it to his brother John.[3] Unfortunately, no date of the transaction is given, but Ernest Frizelle in *The Leicester Royal Infirmary 1771 to 1971* claims that it took place in, or around, 1748, which was just before William entered King's College Medical School, Aberdeen.[4] This date is not borne out by the will of William's brother, John Watts. John's first will, signed on 28 November, 1749, makes no mention of his ownership of Danetts Hall, only his messuages, lands and closes in the Lordship of Bromkinsthorpe. This was an old name for an extra-parochial area of St Mary de Castro, which sat between Braunstone Gate Bridge, Bow Bridge and West Bridge. A codicil to the will, added on 29 July 1759, however, makes it clear that John had by this time moved to the Hall 'John Watts late of the Borough of Leicester and now of Danetts Hall.'[5] John's initial will of 1749 also helps to confirm Samuel Coltman's claim that John and his wife, Joan, lived abroad for a period of time after their marriage:

> Last will and testament of me John Watts lately of the borough of Leicester and about to sail for Kings Town in the island of Jamaica.[6]

It is certain that John and Joan were married when the 1749 will was made as he refers to her as '. . . my dear and tenderly beloved wife Joan Watts'.[7]A daughter, named Joan, was their first child to be baptised at St Mary de Castro on 19 May 1758.[8] Whether, or not, they had any children prior to this is unknown. There may have been another daughter, called Elizabeth, born after Joan, although there is no certainty about this, except that there is some mention of Susanna having two older sisters, who died of tuberculosis in their youth.[9]

Susanna, the last daughter of John and Joan Watts was born on 2 July 1768 with her baptism taking place at St Mary de Castro, when she was only four days old, on 5 July.[10] She was cared for by a nanny, who she makes reference to some forty six years later in a letter written to her friend, Mary Ann Coltman, when away from home and staying at Yoxall Lodge, in the Needwood Forest, in December 1814:

> . . . I know Nanny will be in a fidget about my having so few clothes with me, but tell her for her comfort that I do not fail to make myself very smart for dinner at half-past four, and tell her that my cough is better.[11]

The lasting concern of the nanny may, in some way, be due to the fact Susanna lost her father at a very young age. He died on 15 October 1769, when Susanna was only fifteen months old, plunging his wife and young family into some degree of financial difficulty. There is a hint of the family's declining financial situation in the codicil to her father's will, signed in 1759, some ten years before his death. Here he revokes a bequest, made in 1749, of twenty pounds to be given to his brother William for the purchase of a ring. John states that he is not revoking the bequest 'out of personal pique' but because he feels that his 'family will have more need of the said legacy than I hope my said brother will ever have occasion for.'[12] As a consequence of the financial constraints placed on Joan Watts after her husband's death, she was apparently forced to sell Danetts Hall. Once again there is uncertainty about the date at which this transaction took place. Some accounts claim that it was sold shortly after she was widowed, whereas an obituary for Susanna in the *Leicester Chronicle* claimed that the Hall was not sold until several years after.[13]

Danetts Hall, painted from West Bridge (circa 1800), by Miss Payne.

The identity of Susanna's mother has been somewhat of an enigma. I have been unable to locate her marriage to John Watts, which would have given her maiden name.[14] Her obituary in the *Leicester Journal,* in 1807, gave no biographical details about her own family, or maiden name. It only recorded that she was the widow of John Watts and then continued to give details about the achievements of John Watts's grandfather. The brief biographical sketch of Joan Watts, given in Samuel Coltman's memoirs *Times Stepping Stones* paints a rather negative picture of her, claiming that she was 'an uneducated country girl', who was 'inferior . . . in mind and manners . . .', to her daughter.[15] Following this Samuel continues to make disparaging comments about Joan's character:

> [Her mother] could not habituate herself to the altered circumstances in which Mr Watts . . . had left her – and was constantly referring (like Dicken's Mrs Nickelby) on account of the deprivation of society, and other luxuries, which it was impossible for her daughter, with all her exertions to procure further.[16]

The only part of Samuel Coltman's aspersions about Joan that can really be verified is the fact that she was a country girl. The two clues to her family identity come in the form of two bequests made by Susanna in her will and the presence of a member of Susanna's family, Ann Woodford, of Kibworth Harcourt, who was present at her death.[17] The two bequests were made to Susanna's cousins, Elizabeth Woodford and her sister, Martha Franks.[18] These were the daughters of her aunt and uncle, John and Elizabeth Woodford. Elizabeth and Susanna's mother were sisters who were the daughters of John Clarke and his wife Ann Clarke (nee Bates) of Kibworth Harcourt. Joan was born in June 1731 and Elizabeth in January 1738.[19]

There is no known likeness of Joan Watts surviving in Leicester, although a likeness of her is known to have existed and this is verified by Susanna in her will, in which she makes it a bequest to her friend, Annie Heyrick (nee Greatorex), wife of William Heyrick of Thurmaston. An indication of Joan's appearance in old age, does, however, exist. This description is given in a letter, written by Maria Edgeworth, in September 1803, after visiting the Watts household:

> Mrs Watts, a tall, black-eyed, prim, dragon looking woman . . . after many twistings of her wrists, elbows and neck, all of which appeared to be dislocated fixed herself in her arm-chair, resting her hands on the black mahogany splayed elbows. Her person was no sooner at rest than her eyes and all her features again began to move in all directions. She looked like a nervous and suspicious person electrified.[20]

Joan was clearly suffering from some form of dementia and this had deep and lasting effects on Susanna:

> Miss Watts impression of this fearful calamity clung to her through life, and we believe induced a dread of insanity in her own case, from which she was never after free, though she shrank with painful sensitiveness from ever speaking of it.[21]

The strain of caring for her mother, during the last year of her life, was particularly difficult for Susanna and this period of time was described as the 'winter of adversity'.[22] Susanna did not care for her mother alone, but received help from two women called Sarah Jones and Mary Barkby. Twenty four years following her mother's death Susanna remembered both women in her will:

> It is my will and earnest desire that, if it please God to call me hence, before I shall legally so direct, that Sarah Jones, wife of Robert Jones shall be taken care of as far as the residue of my property shall permit, in consideration of her having been a faithful and disinterested servant to

my mother, in a time of calamity – and also that Mary Barkby – widow of Thomas Barkby be helped as far as may be out of some residue.[23]

Joan's struggle finally came to an end in early May, 1807, when she died, aged 75 years and was buried in the family vault at St Mary de Castro.

Not only had Susanna had the responsibility of caring for her aging, senile mother, but she also experienced the financial responsibility of providing for both of them from quite a tender age. When only fifteen years of age it was discovered that the income from the patrimony left them by her father, John Watts, was practically exhausted. This was probably exacerbated by the fact that her uncle, William Watts, died when she was fifteen. He may have been making some form of financial contribution to assist Susanna and her mother, but then, he, too, '[had had] considerable reverses of fortune and died poor.'[24] The *Leicester Chronicle* states after Susanna's death that '. . . the encumbered property of the family [Danetts Hall] was sold for a small annuity on which she [Susanna] afterwards lived.'[25] In order to bolster the family income, and maintain some degree of gentility, Susanna endeavoured to 'live by the pen.' Nichols tells us that:

> She has distinguished herself as a writer; having, at an early age published 'The Selector' and since then a translation of Telemachus into verse.[26]

Susanna's age at the time of these publications is uncertain, but she was only sixteen when she published a pamphlet entitled *Chinese Maxims* in 1784. Around this time, and later, Susanna seems to have written several poems to mark local and national events. They included a poem, published in the *Leicester Journal,* to mark the Duke of Rutland's twenty first birthday, on the 4 January, 1799; a prologue, rather than a poem for the opening night of Leicester's new theatre, in 1800, and a more politically astringent poem to mark the defeat of Bonaparte. The latter was published in single sheet form and sold to the general public. Verse three shows Susanna's clear contempt for the man:

Bonaparte's Fall

And shall they be silent, when Europe assembled;
Strikes down this Goliath whose impious mind,
Has sought, with ambition and pride undissembled,
To throw one vast fetter around human kind.[27]

Women's writing in the eighteenth century, particularly that of fiction, had increased tremendously, as it was seen as a 'respectable' pastime for middle-class women to engage in. It was also one of only a few ways, albeit a rather precarious one, in which any single, married, or widowed middle class woman could hope to earn an independent living, particularly after a downturn in family fortunes.

Susanna's educational background is not entirely clear, as there is some degree of contradiction with regard to who had taught her. In *A Few Recollections of the Late Miss Susanna Watts* the unknown author claims that:

> Without other instruction than the aid and encouragement of an early old friend, she acquired a thorough knowledge of French and Italian.[28]

The 'old friend' referred to here was possibly Samuel Coltman. For in his memoirs he says that he added to her education by '. . . lending her books and encouraging her . . .'[29] He also claims that her father taught her Italian. The latter statement was impossible, as Susanna's father died on 15 October 1769 when she was only fifteen months old. Her obituary in the *Leicester Chronicle* is, perhaps, more accurate in its claim that she:

> . . . learned French and Italian without the aid of masters and used the powers acquired writing for the booksellers, and thus honourably earned her daily bread.[30]

With no further information about her education available, one is forced to speculate that, as the newspaper suggests, she was largely self-taught. Whatever her education it appears to have been fairly broad in its content and this enabled her to write about a variety of subjects in her publications. Susanna's education, mental ability and her temperament seemed to have earned her considerable local acclaim, if Clara Parkes's comment about her is to be taken seriously:

> Miss Watts was very highly esteemed in her native town for her taste and genius, as well as for her lovely and amiable disposition.[31]

It is difficult to assess the financial input Susanna's writing brought to the family purse, but I would suspect that it was very little, judging by what she published and the rate at which she published. I have found no evidence of any works being published between *Chinese Maxims,* in 1784, and *The Wonderful Travels of Prince Fan-Feredin in the Country of Arcadia,* in 1794. This latter work was translated from the original French and published in Northampton. Following this there seems to have been a publication gap of some eight years until she published *Original Poems and Translations, particularly AMBRA from Lorenzo De Medici,* in 1802. It was sold by all of the booksellers in Leicester, which tends to indicate that it was a popular publication. The majority of the poems were written by Susanna, and apart from some of the smaller pieces, none had previously been published. One of the longer poems by Susanna, entitled *A Forlorn Stranger,* illustrates well her love of nature, particularly trees, and her compassion for their destruction. The words of the poem are supposedly spoken by the last remaining Cedar of Lebanon in the grounds of Quenby Hall. There were originally thought to have been ten cedars on the estate, which were all flourishing, when Shuckbrugh Ashby purchased the Hall in 1770. But after other trees, which were crowding the cedars out, were felled, all but one of the cedars died. Not only did Susanna write about this 'forlorn stranger', but she is also recorded as having made a sketch of it on 24 July, 1801.

Apart from the above mentioned books, Susanna may have published, or written, other works unknown to us between the years 1794 and 1802. One such unknown work is mentioned by Maria Edgeworth in a letter to her relative, Mary Sneyd. She writes 'This poor girl sold a novel in four volumes for ten guineas to Lane.'[32] Unfortunately, no title of the novel is given and there is no indication of whether, or not, it was published. Susanna may have used a pseudonym, rather than her own name, as this was a popular thing to do at the time for women who wished to get into print. William Lane was a publisher at the end of the eighteenth and early nineteenth centuries who actively promoted the production and sale of women's work, particularly that of fiction, through the Minerva Press. There was a tremendous rise in the number of novels being written by women at this time and Susanna obviously hoped to enter the market. According to Cheryl Turner, most women novelists sold their copyright to the publisher, as it was the easiest way to obtain an income from their labours.[33] She further points out that although there was a distinct advantage to a direct sale, there were also disadvantages in that the price paid by the publisher was generally low. It usually amounted to somewhere between five and ten guineas. It would seem that Susanna received the higher amount, but then it was a four volume novel, and had it been published she would never have received any royalties from it having sold the copyright. Maria Edgeworth clearly saw the exploitation involved in this transaction by her further comment on the situation 'Poor girl, that she had no friend to direct her talents; how much she made me feel the value of mine!'[34] It is not surprising that Maria Edgeworth made this comment, for as Dale Spender points out, she was an extremely successful novelist during her heyday, 1800-1814.[35] Her novels were extremely popular and she received unprecedented sums of money for her writing.[36] Marilyn Butler goes as far as to say that apart from Maria there was no other woman, before George Eliot, who had a comparable literary career.[37]

A lack of guidance and advice may have been Susanna's downfall when it came to her major translation of La Gerusalemme (Jerusalem Delivered) by the late Renaissance Italian poet, Torquato Tasso. Shortly before it was due to go to the press, circa 1786, Susanna was rewarded with the news that John Hoole's translation of the same work had been published. She writes of what must surely have been extremely devastating news 'Labour lost – for another translation having appeared a short time before, mine was of no use.'[38] Despite this crushing blow Susanna did receive some acclaim for her epic work. In Mary Pilkington's *Memoirs of Celebrated Female Characters*, published in 1804, there appears the following acknowledgement:

> This lady ranks high in the present list of literary characters, and may justly be considered as the rival of Hoole: she is even allowed to have discovered beauties on that much admired poet Tasso, which that gentleman did not find out.[39]

Maria Edgeworth's letter to Mary Sneyd, in 1802 also reveals recognition of Susanna's translation of Tasso:

> I recollected to have seen some years ago a specimen of this lady's proposed translation of Tasso, which my father had deeply admired.[40]

It is interesting that Richard Edgeworth had had the opportunity to read Susanna's work on Tasso, for, according to Clara Parkes, it was never published. But Clara, like Maria, claims that '. . . by judges who read it, it was pronounced for truthfulness and feeling to be superior to that of Hoole.'[41] Further acknowledgement of Susanna's translation exists in a book of poems by John Heyrick, the husband of Elizabeth Heyrick (nee Coltman). The poems were published shortly after John's untimely death in 1797 and it is the title of the poem which acknowledges Susanna's triumph *Poem to Miss Susanna Watts: The Elegant Translator of Tasso.*[42]

Susanna, however, did not totally escape the effects which the labour and privations of translating and writing were said to have caused. The main effect was a severe head pain 'which . . . had few intervals of ease, even to the close of her long life.'[43] This is confirmed in December 1814 when she bitterly complained of the frustration caused by head pain in a letter to Mary Ann Coltman, when staying at Yoxall Lodge:

> Here is a library full of books, but my head aches so I cannot read with pleasure. Oh! That I had a new head, or that I could manage my old one better, which I am resolved I will try to do. Here are books, and pictures,

and music, and dry gravel walks, a fine large mansion, and good hearts within it, and my stupid head cannot feel as it ought; that is, it cannot worthily enjoy all these good things; but as you say, let us do all we can – angels can do no more.[44]

This health problem in no way prevented Susanna from continuing to write, or publish her work. A brief biographical sketch which appeared in the *Leicester Chronicle* shortly after Susanna's death would have us believe otherwise. It claims that after the failure to publish her translation of Tasso she '. . . gave up writing . . . and devoted herself to the passing interests of the day.' [45]

This was certainly not the case, for as we have already seen, she published her book of *Original Poems and Translations* in 1802. Following this, Susanna's other great work, *A Walk through Leicester: being a Guide to Strangers, containing A Description of the Town and It's Environs with remarks upon its History and Antiquities,* was published in 1804. This guide gives us a tremendous picture of Leicester at the beginning of the nineteenth century and the route she describes can still be walked today. The tour commenced at the Three Crowns Inn in Gallowtree Gate, which she said was 'corruptly pronounced 'Goltre' and ended, after taking in many historical sites and locations, in the Market Place.[46] Some of the roads and buildings mentioned are long since disappeared and some have changed their names. For example, during Susanna's lifetime St Peter's Lane was known as Woman's Lane. She clearly did not approve of this renaming, but says nothing in way of explanation for the change:

> Opposite the Great Meeting is a Meeting House newly erected by a society of Independents, which will seat six hundred persons; and in the adjoining lane, which has undergone a nominal degeneracy from St Peter's Lane to Woman's Lane, is another, erected 1803, by a society calling themselves Episcopalian Baptists.[47]

William Gardiner in his book *Music and Friends,* published in 1838, *does,* however, give an explanation for the renaming of the road. He claims that the change occurred because:

> Two hundred years ago seven poor creatures were burnt in Woman's Lane – from which circumstance it has retained this name until recently.[48]

Susanna had much admiration for her town and county and this can be seen in a poem entitled *Old Leicestershire or The Forty Brothers,* which she had written, circa 1811:

> Of all the brave Counties on England's fair coast
> (Though each may its diff'rent advantages boast)
> The first on the list shall old Leicestershire stand,
> 'Tis the shape of a heart and the heart of the land.[49]

The poem goes on to sing the praises of the town and county, naming amongst other things: Leicestershire's green pastures, its frame-work knitting, Swithland blue slate and the Jewry Wall. Twenty six years later, in October 1837, when writing to Mary Ann Coltman, who had been absent from the town for some time, Susanna is keen to convey new developments taking place in the town:

> Strange alterations are going on in Mr Pares' shrubbery; all the beautiful old limes are felled, except Mr Burgess's, and a new street is to be made out of the Newark below Mr Ryleys into the paddock and a new road from the Hinckley Road to come up the Newarke . . . Four houses have started up like mushrooms since I have been gone, so dear sis. Ann you will see a _new_ old Leicester.[50]

The poem, _Old Leicestershire,_ like the first edition of Susanna's guide to Leicester, was published by Thomas Coombe. In 1799 he took over and expanded the subscription library in Gallowtree Gate, which had been founded in 1790 by Richard Phillips. Another private circulating library had also been established in 1800 by Isaac Cockshaw senior, who had also printed and sold some of Susanna's books and poems. Cheryl Turner in _Living By The Pen_ believes that circulating libraries played a vital role in helping to promote literature, of various types, particularly that of fiction, which was written by a growing number of women in the late eighteenth century. The libraries provided both outlets for publishers and copies of books to either borrow, or buy, for the reader. When Maria Edgeworth came to Leicester in 1802, with her father, they visited a circulating library in the town which could have been either Coombes, or Cockshaws. Whichever bookseller it was, we are told that he was 'an open-hearted man', who 'begged' them to look at a copy of Susanna's recently published poems.[51] I presume this to have been _Original Poems and Translations particularly AMBRA from Lorenzo De Medici,_ which was published in 1802. So keen was the bookseller to promote Susanna's publication that he volunteered to take both Maria and her father to visit Susanna that very same evening:

> When we had dined, we set out with our enthusiastic bookseller. We were shown by the light of a lantern along a very narrow passage

between high walls, to the door of a decent looking house: a maid-servant, candle in hand, received us." Be pleased, ladies to walk upstairs." A neatish room, nothing extraordinary in it, except the inhabitants . . .[52]

Isaac Cockshaw died in 1818, but his circulating library continued to exist and was run by his oldest son, Isaac. A younger son, called Albert, opened an additional library in 1824, adding a reading and news room three years later. Isaac senior had been a drawing master and engraver and possibly moved into the bookselling and library trade when he married Peggy Coombe in 1786. It is not certain, but she may have been Thomas Coombe's daughter, as they named their second son Thomas Coombe Cockshaw. Susanna's relationship with the Cockshaws was not just a business arrangement, for one of her closest friends was Jeanette, the sixth child of Isaac senior and his wife, Peggy. She was a good deal younger than Susanna, being born in 1798, but this does not seem to have mattered. Jeanette ran a women's seminary in Newtown Street and gains entry to Susanna's scrapbook through two very fine drawings. One drawing, dated 11 July 1834, is of the remaining Cedar of Lebanon at Quenby Hall. The

The Cedar of Lebanon, sketched by Jeanette Cockshaw.

other one, dated 9 April 1838, is a sketch of the chamber in which Richard III is said to have slept before the Battle of Bosworth Field. The *Leicester Chronicle's* report on Susanna's funeral names Jeannette as one of Susanna's intimate friends and this is borne out by the bequests made to Jeanette in Susanna's will. They include: five silver tablespoons, eight silver teaspoons, two silver salt spoons, Cowper's poems, a copy of Robert Hall's *Sermons* and a bible which is specifically identified as 'the smaller quarto which I use.'[53]

Evidence of Susanna's other friendships can also be found in various sources. One of her most trusty friends seems to have been of the four legged variety. You can plainly see Susanna's love and admiration for her dog in her poem entitled *A Tribute to My Dog Dash:*

> My dog – a very simple story
> Shall show thy worth with honor due;
> Devoid of all poetic glory,
> And like thyself, plain, honest, true.[54]

The poem appears in her admirable publication *The Animal's Friend.* This book could be either purchased for two shillings and sixpence for the edition bound in cloth, or three shillings and sixpence for one beautifully bound in green silk with an embossed flower design and gold lettering. Dash is also immortalised, at Susanna's side, in the self-portrait which appears in Susanna's scrapbook. Other pets belonging to Susanna, including Keeper, the dog, and the cats, Bigio and Motley, are also immortalised in poetic and prose form in *The Animals Friend.* The book is largely aimed at encouraging children to be kind to insects and animals from a young age. Not only does she see it as morally right, but also a religious duty. She, therefore, instructs parents and children's nurses never to allow children 'to catch and pull in pieces flies and butterflies'.[55] She also warns that a child's early socialisation can lead to unthinking and cruel actions:

> It is common to say to children, "don't touch that nasty creeping thing," and the child ever afterwards will start at a spider, a beetle, or a worm, or stamp upon it and kill it.[56]

Rather than teaching a child to fear and dislike animals and insects she recommends they be encouraged to recognise their value, particularly when saying their prayers:

The child is taught to give thanks for its food, its sleep, etc. and why not instil also, gratitude to God for the sheep which furnish its clothing, the cow that gives its milk, etc.[57]

The opinions Susanna held on the nations cruelty to animals is made very clear in the extended title of another book concerning animal cruelty *A Collection of Observations and Facts Tending to Restrain Cruelty and Inculcate Kindness Towards Animals,* and in the biting and forthright manner in which she writes on page one:

> It is a very striking fact, that though the present age is boasted as highly enlightened, refined, and as far removed from barbarism as science, art and literature can make it, no nation which we call savages, practices more degrading cruelty towards animals than the people of Great Britain.[58]

Susanna's concern for the animal kingdom is extended even further in 1828 when she published a further book entitled *The Insects in Council: Addressed to Entomologists with other Poems.* Her intension for publishing here was:

> The following little Fable is not presented to the Public as a bagatelle of amusement suggested by the fashionable popularity of Entomology, but under a serious, anxious, and most sincere desire to inculcate respect and tenderness towards all the inferior creatures.[59]

Susanna shared her concern for the health and well-being of animals with her close friend, Elizabeth Heyrick. She, too, had written on the subject, particularly that of bull-baiting. Susanna's friendship with Elizabeth was extended to the whole of the Coltman family of St Nicholas Street.  Evidence of this can be found in Samuel Coltman's memoirs *Times Stepping Stones.* Here he not only writes very affectionately of Susanna, but he also reveals the family name for her, which is 'Sister Sue'.[60] This family friendship lasted for sixty years and their pet name, admiration and love for her is confirmed in the last letter sent by Samuel's mother, Elizabeth Coltman, when frail in old age, to her daughter, Mary Ann.

> . . . I don't know when I have been better than I am now; although they take very good care of me . . . daughter Susan is also very kind; to-day she is not at home, but thy letter is left for her to read.[61]

The section of Samuel's memoirs, entitled *Some of the Ladies of Leicester at the Close of the Eighteenth Century,* reveals the close bond of friendship that was formed between Susanna, his two sisters Elizabeth and Mary Ann, and others:

> Three intimate friends of my sisters, who had minds highly cultivated, manners refined, according to the fashion of those days; and characters, which, charming as they were in youth, became in their mature days elevated and distinguished.[62]

The three intimate friends were Elizabeth Coltman of the Newarke (who was not related to the Coltman's of St Nicholas Street), Mary Reid, (daughter of Matthew Reid, a hosier and draper in the Market Place), and, of course, 'Sister Sue', who was, by all accounts 'a greater favourite than either of the [other] two.'[63]. It seems to have been an intellectual, exclusively female group, if Susanna's poem *Lines – To the Reverend Robert Throsby,* written in 1800, are any indication. The poem was written in response to him:

. . . saying that a Party of Ladies who had established a little Book Society were a <u>set of Dragons</u>, because they refused to admit him to their meetings.[64]

A grave Divine accustomed oft to view
With longing eye, our meetings of Bas<u> bleu,</u>
Himself excluded, in an angry pet,
Baptised this learned Club, <u>a Dragon set.</u> –

We own, good Sir, your simile is keen; -
Perchance you think to rouse our female spleen.-
Not so! – Your judgement we politely trust,
And, with a curtsey, own th' allusion <u>just.</u>

A Dragon is by Naturalist's Defined,
A wondrous creature of the <u>Serpent</u> kind;
And serpents – Holy Writ this truth supplies,
Are ever deemed an emblem of <u>The Wise</u>;
Vast <u>wings</u> they spread – and these you'll not deny,
Are <u>Fancy's pinions</u>, form'd to soar on high;-

Their <u>tongues</u> are <u>forky</u> – here the truth you hit;
For sure, a <u>pointed tongue</u> denotes <u>a Wit</u>;
They <u>vomit flames</u>,- your simile is here,
By ev'ry rule of rhetoric strong and clear;-
For see you not – how from our mouths transpire
Huge blazing volumes of <u>poetic fire</u>?-

Thanks, flattering Sir – you give us much to Brag on
I sign (for all) – the illustrious Name

A Dragon.[65]

Robert Throsby was the cousin of the Tory and Anglican local historian, John Throsby. Whether, or not, he received a copy of the poem is unknown, but it does make very interesting reading, as Susanna cleverly turns his chastisement, with some mirth, into a compliment and by so doing shows the group to have

The Reverend Robert Throsby (circa 1800).

adopted the badge of 'Bas bleu' with pride. The original 'Bas bleu' literary society was formed by the educated Parisian hostess, Mme de Polignac in the 1590s. This, and later such societies, played their part in influencing eighteenth century ideas about women's education. For example, in the 1750s the wealthy London hostess, Elizabeth Montague, in trying to escape the tedium of 'accomplishments', mindless card playing and tedious conversation, held soirees for women, to which men would be invited for intellectual discussion. One of the men regularly invited was the amateur poet, Benjamin Stillingfleet, who always wore the grey, or blue, worsted stockings of domestic life, rather than the black silk stockings of social life that etiquette demanded. Hence the women attending these gatherings became known as Bluestockings. Montague and many of her friends, male and female, like the Leicester trio, gladly adopted the badge of Bas bleu. However, by the time Susanna's circle of female friends met the term, 'Bas bleu' had acquired a totally pejorative meaning and was used to refer to women who were thought to ape men by affecting to understand intellectual and literary matters. Consequently, such women became the butt of criticism and were suspected of 'unnatural longings'. But Susanna and her friends seem to have risen above the term's negative connotation and wore the badge of the 'Bas bleu' with pride. They also adopted the imagery of the dragon and serpent as being positive symbols of womanhood and learning.

In Susanna's scrapbook there are several pictures of women known to be Bluestockings, including one of Hannah More (1745-1833). Hannah was one of the later generations of Bluestockings, although she is documented as holding very politically conservative views about society in general and women, in particular. She, for example, believed in the importance of women's subordination and stressed the benefits of obedience, patience and humility. However, she did help to expand the role of philanthropy for women and engaged in the debate on improving women's education. Other pictures of Bluestockings include: Hester Chapone, the author of educational books, Sarah Trimmer, the writer and historian, Mrs Benger and the philanthropist and writer, Priscilla Wakefield. Priscilla's best selling book was *The Juvenile Travellers,* which was a description of an imaginary tour through Europe. Between 1801 and 1850 it went through nineteen editions. It was, perhaps, this book that gave Susanna inspiration to write her guide to Leicester. Her guide about a real town, rather than an imaginary tour through a continent, can be likened to Priscilla's book in that it is a tour which is written for imaginary people who might be visiting the town:

> To the traveller who may wish to visit whatever is deemed most worthy of notice in the town of Leicester. . .We now request our good-humoured stranger to accept of such our guidance; whether he be the tourist, whose object of inquiry is general information – or the man of reflection, who, wherever he goes, whether in crowded towns or solitary fields, finds something to engage his meditation – or the mercantile rider, who, when the business of his commission is transacted, quits his lonely parlour for a stroll through the streets – we shall endeavour to bring before his eyes as much of interest as our scenes will afford: and for the diligent antiquary, we assure him we will make the most of our Roman remains; and we hope he will not quarrel with the rough forest stones of our

streets, when we promise him they shall conduct him to the smoother pavement of Roman mosaic.[66]

Bluestockings, clockwise from top left: Sarah Trimmer, Hester Chapone, Hannah More and Priscilla Wakefield.

The pictures of Bluestockings pasted into Susanna's scrapbook were presumably women that Susanna admired and looked to as role models. She, no doubt, hoped that she would, one day, attain the same level of writing success.

To return to Susanna's friendships, it would seem that they were of immense importance to her and she makes this very clear in a poem written on the subject:

A Friend

Say, which is the chiefest of blessings below,
Which charms us in joy and supports us in woe,
On which our best comforts must ever depend?-
Our hearts answer truly – "That blessings a Friend.
Say, which is the chiefest of blessings above,
The source of our Faith, be our Hope and our Love?-
Tis a Friend – yes, that Friend who is "Mighty to save"
And who will be by our side thro' the gloom of the Grave.[67]

Friends feature highly in Susanna's scrapbook, but there is no mention of living family members from either her father's, or mother's side. Even her famous uncle, William Watts, who promoted the establishment of the infirmary in Leicester, is not mentioned, but Susanna was only fifteen at the time of his death. She did, however, maintain some sort of link with the Watts family, in that William's grandson, William Mosley Watts, born three months before his grandfather's death, inherited from Susanna the Watts family pictures and seals, plus a damask table cloth and napkins.[68] His sister, Anastasia, according to Susanna's initial will of 1824, was to have received a legacy of ten pounds, but this bequest was later revoked in a codicil made in 1840. Apart from two further small bequests to cousins from her mother's side, Susanna's will reflects the importance of friends and servants over family. The companionship and support they gave her are remembered and rewarded with treasured artefacts and practical objects, which are specifically named in her will. The executor of her will, for example, was not a family member, but 'her much valued friend' William Heyrick of Thurmaston Lodge. He was the brother of John Heyrick, who had been married to her close friend Elizabeth Heyrick. For his executor services and friendship William received a needlework picture of Emma, which had won Susanna a silver medal from the Society of Arts. This he eventually bequeathed to one of his sisters. William's wife, Annie, was bequeathed a miniature picture of Susanna's mother, which normally, one might have thought, would have been given to a surviving member of Susanna's mother's family.

Another friend to receive a bequest from Susanna's will was Ellen Alexander (nee Waterhouse) who was the wife of Dr Edward Alexander of Danetts Hall. She was to receive one of Susanna's feather pictures, but this was never to be as Ellen died in December 1826, some four years after her husband. Like many middle class women of the time Susanna had been quite accomplished in creating artistic forms from feathers. According to Clara Parkes this artistic work also extended to working with hair:

> She [Susanna] gained a medal from a Society for encouraging art, for an ingenious kind of needle-work in hair and she invented a mode of designing landscapes of feathers, which were very curious and beautiful.[69]

Ellen and Edward Alexander had bought Danetts Hall in 1804 and, it would seem that they became close friends with Susanna. In November 1810 Susanna's compassion for the destruction of trees surfaced again when she wrote Ellen Alexander a seven verse poem of consolation '. . .when a violent storm had blown down one of the elms by the gate of Danetts Hall and shattered another which was carefully propped and repaired.'[70] Four years later, in 1814, Susanna displays her true devotion to her friends at Danetts Hall when she writes to Mary Ann Coltman:

> Pray (but I need not ask you) set off to Danetts Hall directly, to carry thither my love and duty and wishes and prayers, and tell my kind friends I long to see them.[71]

Apart from the Alexanders, Susanna's will discloses many other friends who were recipients of her possessions. A Mrs Foster received a piece of Susanna's needlework in addition to two blue china ornaments, Mrs Mansfield a china teapot and stand and Mary Ann Coltman, Susanna's writing desk. Several other friends received copies of Susanna's books, each title being named by her on a memorandum attached to the will. One of the recipients was Eleanor Frewen Turner (nee Clarke), who was married to John Frewen Turner, Lord of the Manor of Cold Overton. It is uncertain how the friendship between Susanna and Eleanor began, but it appears to have been a very close one. In 1822 both seem to have either belonged to, or supported, the Leicester Ladies Committee, which at that time was fund raising for the 'Distressed Irish'. The *Leicester Journal* gave the following report on the situation in Ireland in October 1822:

> Wretched state of the peasantry in the South and West of Ireland – they have parted with almost all aspects of clothing in order to purchase food and are now in a state of nakedness.[72]

The Committee asked for all donations and parcels of clothing to be left at the Female Asylum in the Newarke. Susanna and Eleanor were listed as two of the people who donated clothing parcels with Eleanor asking that it be made known that hers consisted of many articles which were made gratis by the cottagers of Cold Overton.[73] In 1830 both women again became involved in fund raising for the Irish, when they responded to an appeal from Maria Edgeworth. This time they tried to sell straw bonnets to aid distressed Irish women. Their attempts were largely unsuccessful, as explained by Susanna in a letter to Maria:

> Mrs Frewen Turner with indefatigable energy, used all her influence to promote the sale of the bonnets in the county, in London, in Bath and in various other parts of England. Myself and other friends exerted ourselves in this town and county; but all was ineffectual. The Bonnets received from the manufactory patronized by Mr Duckworth were very defective and would not make their way by their own merit. Those which were sold, were bought by friends merely to forward the cause . . . all our exertions have not enabled us to procure one sixpence more than the £13.11.0, which I remitted to [Mr Duckworth] some time ago. The remaining bonnets are neither wearable, nor saleable, having been tried and exposed a long time in shops and many of them being so small in the crown as to be unfit for children.[74]

A further venture into fund raising, by Susanna and Eleanor, came in 1838, when they both became involved with efforts to establish the Leicester Lunatic Asylum. Susanna captures their efforts in a poem entitled, *The Bosom Friend*. 'Bosom Friends' were knitted articles that covered the top half of the body and these were sold in aid of the Asylum at a bazaar in the grounds of Overton Hall. In the following extract from the poem Susanna makes it clear when the 'bosom friend' should be worn:

> I am no summer friend – not I –
> That changes with each varying sky.-
> I court you not when suns are bright,
> And modestly retire from sight;
> But when cold blasts shall chill your frame
> I'll then my faithful office claim,
> To cheer you mid the wintry storm,
> A comforter both tried and warm. -
> So take me to your bosom, pray –
> Its secrets I shall never betray.-[75]

During the year 1826, at a cost of two thousand pounds, John Frewen Turner, husband of Eleanor, founded an Asylum for female orphans in Cold Overton. Its aim was to provide a home and education for twenty girls. It is impossible to know to what extent, if any, Susanna was involved with this venture, but being such a close friend of Eleanor there was, more than likely, some involvement. It may have been a child from this institution, or one of the young children that she is said to have taught after the death of her mother, that Susanna adopted, but there is no mention of an adopted child in her will.[76]

Susanna and Eleanor's friendship also extended into the abolitionist cause. Susanna's other friends, Elizabeth Heyrick, Mary Ann Coltman and Elizabeth Coltman, were also deeply engaged. In 1824 they canvassed the people of Leicester to boycott slave grown sugar, persuading them instead to use, and sell, sugar from the East India Sugar Company. By June the following year they were successful in achieving the following results:

> In the town of Leicester, by the zeal and activity of a very *few* individuals alone, nearly one fourth of the population, viz.1500 families have been so impressed by the subject, as to engage themselves to abstain from the use of West-Indian sugar.[77]

Picture of a slave pasted into Susanna's scrapbook.

During 1824 Elizabeth Heyrick anonymously published her now famous pamphlet *Immediate, not Gradual Abolition; or, an Inquiry into the Shortest, Safest, and Most Effectual Means of Getting Rid of West-Indian Slavery.* In this frank and lively written pamphlet Elizabeth called for an end to the policy of amelioration and gradual abolition, which had been espoused by the Anti-Slavery Society when formed in 1823. In order to promote their abolitionist views even further Susanna and two friends launched a periodical called *The Humming Bird or Morsels of Information on the Subject of Slavery with various Miscellaneous Articles,* in December of 1824. One of Susanna's two friends was almost certainly, Elizabeth Heyrick. The other friend was either Mary Ann Coltman, sister of Elizabeth Heyrick, or, Elizabeth Coltman. Hazarding a guess it was probably Mary Ann Coltman. For when they are describing themselves, the third member of the 'triple union' is said to be the youngest and the one who loves to travel. Mary Ann was certainly younger than Susanna and Elizabeth and she did travel quite extensively. The editors of the periodical were particularly concerned for the female slave and this is shown in their 'Address to the Ladies of Great Britain':

> The extremist state of wretchedness to which females can be reduced in our country, poverty, personal hardships, cruel treatment from savage husbands, is far, immeasurably far, above the abyss of degradation in which the female negro-slaves are engulfed. They are under the absolute, unrestrained power of their masters, or as they are termed in the colonies, their owners . . . They have no one right in themselves – body, heart and soul are their owners. Nay even life – if that owner be cruel and vindictive; as even for murdering them, he will only, in some colonies, pay a fine.[78]

Articles like the one above were interspersed with a wide range of articles on other topics, in the hope that the periodical would attract a wide readership. Slipped in amongst these articles were various quotations and definitions, such as one for the word negro 'A creature treated like a brute because he is black, by greater brutes, who happen to be white'.[79]

Like Elizabeth Heyrick's pamphlet, published earlier in 1824, the editors of *The Humming Bird* also wished to remain anonymous. The editorial address to the readership, in the first copy of *The Hummingbird,* clearly states their united female stand, which was impervious to any male hostility:

> . . . We, being an ancient Sisterhood, chuse to follow old ways; and so singular are we in this respect, that we have never been known to adopt any new mode, either in our dress, habits or sentiments, though the date

of our birth is Anno Mundi, one. Since that period we have been united so that "No man may put us asunder," or, by any power or art whatsoever, interrupt our triple union.[80]

Here they claim their 'triple unity' began the year after the world's creation. What stronger bond could they have had? Their forcefulness and determination is again aired and reinforced in a later edition of *The Humming Bird* when responding to a letter of encouragement:

The Humming Bird thus encouraged, feels her native bravery stimulated to double exertion, and she will now, in defence of her brood, not only defy birds ten times larger than herself, but fearlessly encounter even the talons of the vulture.[81]

This united sisterly stand is obviously as strong and forceful as it was earlier in the century when the 'sisterhood' responded to Robert Throsby's attempts to belittle them.

The reason for choosing *The Humming Bird* as the title for the periodical is to contrast the difference between the life of the slave and the bird:

. . . deep and wide is the contrast between a gang of slaves driven to their labour by the harsh crack of the whip, or torn from their wives and children, and the little Humming Bird buzzing like a feathered bee, free and happy to her voluntary labour, or nursing her tiny pearly eggs in security.[82]

In addition to this explanation, Susanna also wrote a song to convey the message and horrors of slavery:

As the small Bird, that flutt'ring roves
Among Jamaica's tam'rind groves,
    A feather'd busy Bee,
In note scarce rising to a song,
Incessant, hums the whole day long,
    In Slavery's Island, free!

So shall "A still small voice" be heard,
Tho' humble as the Humming Bird,
    In Britain's groves of oak;
And to the Peasant from the King,
In ev'ry ear shall ceaseless sing
"Free Afric from the yoke!"[83]

THE HUMMING BIRD. { Composed by Mrs W. Heyrick
The Words by Susanna Watts

The words of the song appear on the editorial page and further on in the
periodical they are accompanied by a musical score, written by Susanna's

friend, Annie Heyrick. There is a slight difference between the two versions of the song in that the word 'tamarind' is exchanged for 'plantain'. This may have been used as a play on words to emphasize the restrictions placed on slaves. The word plantain could either have meant the fruit which is a member of the banana family, or a type of low growing plant that produces seeds which are fed to caged birds, the latter possibly being used as an analogy for the constrained life of the slave. The song and musical score could also be purchased separately for the price of three pence. Like today, songs were a very popular form of expressing protest. When a large proportion of the population was illiterate songs could be learnt and act as a form of conveying news and protest to a wide number of people. This was clearly the purpose of the song being sold in sheet form.

Unfortunately, the publication of *The Humming Bird,* despite obvious support, with words like 'Be of good cheer, the mouse rescued the ensnared lion by only nibbling at the net'[84] only lasted eleven months and a warning of its demise was given, along with thanks to those who supported the women's efforts, in the preface of the first edition:

> We cannot permit the Humming Bird to take wing, and wander beyond the rather narrow circle to which it has hitherto been confined without expressing to those friends who have listened to its unpretending song with indulgent attention, and particularly to those by whose kind aid its existence has been sustained throughout the year. We are the more anxious to make this acknowledgement, as it will probably be our only opportunity of doing so, since increasing infirmities have so far enfeebled the hand of one who took an active part in the work, as to render its future regular appearance doubtful; at present, however, it will not be altogether relinquished.[85]

Another indication of the groups failing health came in the June issue of the *Humming Bird:*

> . . . we have conducted our "Humming Bird" to the half of one year's experience. We faint not in courage, but we may faint in *power*: the ability of mental exertion, however comparatively small, may not keep pace with the wishes of unabated perseverance. Therefore, with a steady, deliberate determination not to desert our post, while we can raise even a palsied arm in defence of our African brethren, we appeal and we appeal *confidently* to the BENEVOLENT, the GIFTED, the ZEALOUS, and the FAITHFUL, for *further literary assistance.*[86]

In April 1825, Elizabeth Heyrick took a further step along the abolitionist path when she became treasurer at the inaugural meeting of the Female Society for the Relief of the British Negro Slaves (renamed The Ladies Negro Friendly Society). Thirteen resolutions were passed at this meeting, each one pledging to fight for the abolition of slavery. The Society's first report stated that:

> A few individuals who commiserated the unhappy condition of British Negro Slaves, and wished to "remember those in bonds, as bound with them", and who particularly felt for the degraded condition of their own sex, ranked as they are in the West Indian Colonies, with the beasts of the field – determined to endeavour to awaken (at least in the bosom of English women) a deep and lasting compassion, not only for the bodily suffering of female slaves, but for their moral degradation . . .[87]

Apart from the normal financial duties of a treasurer, it was also their responsibility to inform the wealthy about the conditions under which the slaves, particularly the women, were living and working in the West Indies, hence the formation of local branches. The Leicester Ladies Anti-Slavery Society branch was formed in June 1825. Susanna and her maid, Mary Brown, were two of the initial eighteen subscribers to the branch.[88] Other names included: Eleanor Frewen Turner of Cold Overton, Mrs S. Coltman, Mrs Cockshaw, Mrs Dicey of Claybrooke Hall and Mrs Ellis of Beaumont Leys.[89] Compared to other local branches, at this time, Leicester was one of the largest, along with Birmingham and West Bromwich. Another branch was formed in Oakham during the same year and Susanna became its vice president, with Hannah Hawley as president and a Mrs Tomblin Keal as treasurer. Mrs Keal was most probably Sarah Keal, nee Tomblin, who was married to William Keal, a surgeon, apothecary and man-midwife, who lived in the Market-Place, Oakham. Hannah Hawley, a Quaker, also lived in the Market-Place. When she died, in 1833, Susanna, wishing to honour her life and work, wrote a ten verse poem, entitled *On the Death of Mrs Hannah Hawley of Oakham*. A copy of the poem has survived in Susanna's scrapbook, but unfortunately records of the Leicester and Oakham branches of the Ladies Anti-Slavery Society do not appear to have survived. However, Susanna's poetic contribution, *The Slaves Address*, which demonstrated the plight of slave mothers, has survived by being used to head up the 1828 annual reports of the Birmingham and Calne branches of the Society:

> Think, how naught but death can sever
> Your lov'd children from your hold;
> Still alive – but lost forever –
> Ours are parted, bought and sold![90]

Active women abolitionists were generally not approved of by many of the male anti-slavers, William Wilberforce being no exception. He expressed his dislike of the Female Society for the Relief of the British Negro Slaves, believing that ' . . . for ladies to meet, to publish, to go from house to house stirring up petitions were things unsuited to the female character, as delineated in Scripture.'[91] This opinion in no way curbed the efforts of the women members, it only made them more resolved to fight for their cause. Susanna made clear, once again by the use of verse, her response to male criticism and opposition:

William Wilberforce

On a Gentleman saying that
Some ladies, who were zealous in the Anti-Slavery Cause, were <u>brazen faced.</u>
Thanks for your thought – it seems to say,
When ladies walk in Duty's way,
They should wear <u>arms of proof;</u>
To blunt the shafts of manly wit –
To ward off censure's galling
And keep reproach aloof:-
And when a <u>righteous cause</u> demands
The labour of their hearts and hands,
Right onward they must pass
Cas'd in strong armour, for the field –
With casque and corselet, spear and shield,
Invulnerable brass.[92]

Although Susanna opposed Wilberforce's beliefs that women should not be publically active in the abolitionist cause, she was associated with him through her friends. As previously pointed out, she had stayed with one of Wilberforce's closest friends, Thomas Gisborne of Yoxall Lodge. She had also been associated with another of his closest friends, Thomas Babington of Rothley Temple. Thomas had married Jean Macaulay, the sister of Aulay Macaulay, who was married to Elizabeth Heyrick's sister-in-law, Ann Heyrick. Thomas Babington and his brother-in-law, Zachary Macaulay, were actively involved in the abolitionist cause. Both were members of the Clapham Circle (so named because many of the members lived near to Clapham Common) and Thomas Babington had been at St John's College, Cambridge, at the same time as Wilberforce. He had also unofficially acted as Wilberforce's parliamentary private secretary for several years. Wilberforce was, therefore, often the guest of the Babingtons at Rothley Temple. Indeed he is thought to have developed part of his abolition motion whilst staying at the Temple in late 1791:

> It was in the groves of Rothley Temple that Mr Thomas Babington and
> Mr Wilberforce drew up the statement of 2000 pages of the cruelties
> practised in the inhuman traffic of slaves.[93]

There is some reference in Susanna's scrapbook to Wilberforce and there is a picture of him. There are also several references to the Babingtons and the Macaulays, along with some mementos from her visits to Rothley Temple. There is, for example, a hymn written by Thomas Babington on 19 March 1833, when Eleanor Frewen, her daughter, Selina, and Susanna were visiting. There is also a picture of Rothley Temple, sketched by Selina Frewen in 1836 and the conclusion of the sermon preached in Cossington Church on the death of Thomas Babington in November,1837.

Susanna had links with other male abolitionists. William Heyrick, her close friend and the executor of her will, was also an abolitionist. At a public meeting, in the New Hall, Wellington Street, on 29 October, 1834, held in aid of the presentation of prayer books to emancipated slaves, William Heyrick was elected president and invited to take the chair.[94] Elizabeth Heyrick's parents and brothers, with whom Susanna was very close, were also abolitionists. John was apparently more in tune and sympathetic to Elizabeth's beliefs than was her other brother, Samuel.

Susanna's abolitionist efforts continued unswervingly up until slavery became abolished throughout the British Colonies with the passing of the Emancipation Act in 1833, which took effect from 1 August 1834. In 1833 she was directly involved with collecting signatures for the London Female Anti-Slavery Society's nation-wide petition against slavery. This was presented to both the House of Commons and the Lords. The number of signatures gathered countrywide amounted to 179,000 for the petition to the Lords and 187,000 for the House of Commons. Signatures gathered in Leicester reached the figure of 3,025, 'time not allowing more' as commented by Susanna.[95]

Not all of the four friends, Susanna, Elizabeth Coltman, Elizabeth Heyrick and Mary Ann Coltman lived to see the Emancipation Bill of August 1833 come into force the following August. Elizabeth Heyrick died, aged 62 years, on 18 October 1831. Her passing was marked by Susanna in the way she felt best able to express her grief and give acknowledgement to Elizabeth's long standing commitment and hard work for the abolitionist cause. She wrote a seven verse poem entitled, *To the Memory of Elizabeth Heyrick*.

The picture used to head a series of hymns adapted for the celebration.

On 1 August 1834 when the Emancipation Act came into effect there was public rejoicing and street celebrations in Leicester. Susanna marked the occasion by writing and publishing a hymn, the proceeds of which were given to a public fund for the rebuilding of places of worship in Jamaica. In the hymn she does not tread lightly when blaming England for its role in the slave trade:

ENGLAND! The sin was thine! – for thou
Didst first their necks to bondage bow,
    Didst steal – and flog – and chain! –
Weep tears of joy! That now imprest
By Heav'ns high impulse on thy breast,
JUSTICE and MERCY stand confest! –
    England's herself again![96]

A tribute to Susanna's unswerving commitment to the abolitionist cause was paid to her posthumously in two known sources:

In later life 'giving all her powers in earnest exertion on behalf of the degraded slave'. In this noble cause she wrote, and thought, and prayed.[97]

During the agitation of the Slavery Question she and her friend Elizabeth Heyrick were indefatigable in the use of their pens and their influence on the side of philanthropy. Their names were illuminated in their native town on the occasion of the liberation of the slaves, in 1834; Elizabeth Heyrick as "the undaunted, persevering and eloquent advocate of 'Immediate not Gradual Abolition'" and Susanna Watts as "The warm hearted defender of oppressed humanity, the succourer of the destitute, and the animal's friend."[98]

When the Emancipation Act came into force Susanna was sixty six years old. Despite her age she seems to have remained active in various charitable causes and political issues. In the very same year she became involved in raising monies for the establishment of infant schools in Leicester. To encourage donations she wrote and published a poem, entitled *The Saviours Command: An Appeal on Behalf of the Infant Schools*. A copy of the poem was pasted into her scrapbook, along with the information that two hundred and forty pounds were raised for the building of the schools at a bazaar held between the 25 and 29 of September.[99] Four infant schools were subsequently built in Archdeacon Lane, Metcalf Street, Charlotte Street and Oxford Street, during the year 1838. In a more reflective mood, on 10 January 1834, she wrote a poem that gives the reader a wonderful insight into her wit, possessions and simple domestic life. The poem is entitled *Scraps of My Brain - Inventory of the Furniture of my Table*. Although it is a lengthy poem, I have included it in full because of the way in which it plays on the imagination:

A Writing Desk, of Daily use,
With ink & wax & quill of goose,
And bills of taxes, coals & candles;-
Which had, but which has not, two handles.-

A Leather Case , full room allotting
For writing paper & for blotting;
For Letters priz'd, from absent friends,
And hints of thoughts, in odds & ends,
On what, in crazy heads despite,
I mean, some future time to write.

Two Books, not small, - in quarto royal,
To keep accounts, all just and loyal.

Another, Wondrous Book indeed!
For Memories that a flapper need;

That tells Arabia's figur'd science,
Yet sets all labour at Defiance;
And teaches those who have no sense,
To reckon shillings, pounds & pence
In less of time than mere enough
To take the smallest pinch of snuff!-

Cats; extra size, & two in number,
Profoundly sunk in peaceful slumber.

A Bag – not such as, rich & rare
Adorns the arm of ladies fair,
With shining clasp & tassels gay,
And broider'd flowers, in sweet array;-
But rusty – and, if truth were told,
A quarter of a century old.-
This bag might say –"I well can show
The ups and downs of all below!
Time was, when I was fresh and young,
I on a Lady's shoulder hung;
She wore a velvet short Pelisse,
Of which, a sleeve, I made a piece;
I was fring'd with lace, so rich to view,
And lin'd with silk of golden hue.
- And here I am – pray notice that,
Companion to this old black cat! –
And Mistress oft times cannot see
Difference twixt Bigio & me;
Tho' Bigio's coat, so sleek and fine,
Is far more velvet-like than mine.
Yet do I not repine – but boast
That of all Bags I'm honour'd most! –
I am no "Bag with holes" – I hold
Bright silver & imperial gold! –
Good Friends extend their "precious palms",
And stove me with their generous alms.
Long may my services endure!
For I can feel for "Aged Poor."
And ne'er will I in duty lag,
But prove a trusty, stout old bag."

Among these matters multifarious,
Are other items, odd and various;-
Perchance a saucer full of crumbs,
For tuneful Robin when he comes.
Perchance, a tray with slice of meat,
For times, when there's no time to eat.

Me thinks you cry – "Your table's bound
As vast as Arthur's Table Round." –
Not so – It holds all these & more,
Yet scarcely stands three feet by four;
And underneath good space provides
For <u>Dash</u> to stretch his ample sides.

Then all is cleared before 'tis dark,
For fear of that Dread thing – a spark!
Then Motley's legs find ample room,-
And Mistress, thankful for the gloom,
Supine upon the sofa lies,
And tries to think - & shuts her eyes.-

Oh happy she, who clearly thinks!
Whose thoughts ne'er run in broken links!
Yet, if the faint ideas lie
Mid cobwebs, like the entangled fly,
They can do neither good nor ill –
Mere harmless nothings – without will.

Now, Heaven be praised! – (if not profane
To end this light & trifling strain
With serious thought) – Yes, Heaven be prais'd!
Who thus my lot in Mercy rais'd;
And "spread my table" for my good,
With humble work and humble food;
And, for my soul's and body's health,
Sav'd me from poverty and wealth! -[100]

Part of the poem empathises with the plight of the elderly and this is understandable because Susanna founded the Society for the Relief of Indigent Old Age, in circa 1828. She remained its secretary and treasurer until 1840. The annual reports, written by Susanna, for the Society, were said to '. . . do honour to her eloquence and piety'.[101] The poem also gives the reader a clue to one of Susanna's habits, the taking of snuff. Many women of her time, including Elizabeth Heyrick, were well practised in the art of snuff-taking. Without her usual quota, when staying at Yoxall Lodge, in December 1814, Susanna wrote, almost in desperation to her friend, Mary Ann Coltman:

> But you must know, Sister Ann, though surrounded with all these charms, I feel like a ship on the Great Pacific, whose crew is reduced to short allowance, for though all comforts, and to me luxuries, are to be found here, there is no _snuff_ in the forest, and my stock is very low; at this you will be wicked enough to rejoice![102]

Although the poem does not specifically relate to Susanna's wearing apparel it does make mention of her twenty five year old bag. Its age tends to indicate that she was either very attached to it, too poor to purchase a new one, not concerned about keeping up with the fashions of the day, or not extravagant in dress. She was certainly opposed to vanity and extravagance of dress and this can be seen in several of the comments she makes throughout her scrapbook. On one occasion, in 1829, she expressed her views, both pictorially and in verse:

A Proverb

In days of yore, when books were few,
And men <u>made use</u> of what they knew;
A <u>scrap</u> of sense was highly priz'd,
And <u>proverbs</u> were not then, despised:
For much good sense & useful lore
Are found in Sancho's favourite store.-
    Fair Ladies! - who, as Mode impels,
Float in your sleeves of full <u>two ells</u>,
You give the Flatterers ample leave-
They may, with ease, <u>creep up your sleeve</u>![103]

When Susanna reached the age of seventy two, in 1840, she is known to have become involved with the politics of church rates. During the 1830s Leicester's dissenters grew increasingly opposed to the payment of church rates. Every householder, whether they belonged to the Church of England, or a Non-Conformist denomination, had, by law, to pay whatever rate was levied by the church vestry of the parish they resided in. If they refused to pay, the churchwardens could prosecute them and order items of their property to be seized and sold at a public auction, in order that the rates could be paid. St Martin's churchwardens were particularly zealous in enforcing the payment of its church rates and this resulted, in 1840, in a leading Leicester dissenter, William Baines, being prosecuted for non-payment of the church rates. After a protracted case he was eventually sentenced to serve seven months in the County Gaol. There was extensive opposition in the town following his sentence and many letters of support for his actions appeared in the *Leicestershire Mercury*. A well attended public meeting, in favour of his cause, was also held at the Theatre Royal, but such action did not deter St Martin's vestry from taking similar action again the following year, whilst William Baines was still in prison. This time four leading dissenters, including Albert Cockshaw, who had often called for the disestablishment of the Church of England, were summonsed for refusing to pay their church rates. They stood firm in their resolution not to pay, but the matter was resolved when their rates were paid for them. Albert's rates were paid by an anonymous person, who turned out to be Susanna. This was confirmed by the *Leicestershire Mercury* which printed that '. . . she paid it without Mr Cockshaw's knowledge; and her high character places the statement beyond all doubt.'[104] Jack Simmons believed that Susanna, although elderly and

Reverend Robert Hall.

short of money, paid Albert's fine. He also thought that because she was a strict Anglican she feared that the Church of England would suffer further if it made martyrs out of these men, like it had with William Baines.[105] The fact that she feared for the position of the Church of England may well have been the case, but there are possibly other reasons for her actions, too. Susanna may have been a zealous church woman, but she also seems to have had some sympathies with the dissenters. In her scrapbook there is a picture of the Reverend Robert Hall and part of a sermon which she heard him preach, at Harvey Lane Chapel, on Wednesday evening, 27 September, 1820. In addition to this, she owned a copy of *Robert Hall's Sermons*. One has to remember here, that Robert Hall, as Florence Skillington rightly points out:

. . . was one of the greatest pulpit orators of the age, and no barrister, member of parliament, or person of fashion passing through Leicester missed the opportunity of hearing him; indeed, some travelled from London for the purpose.[106]

In addition to Hall, Susanna also pays homage to William Carey, the Baptist preacher and missionary, when writing to her friend, Mary Ann Coltman:

Pray have you seen 'Dr Carey's Life'? It is written by his nephew, Eustace. I do so long to see it! The shoemaker of Leicester becoming the great Eastern linguist and the true disciple of Christ! What a man! Your dear father and mother knew him well (and had their shoes mended by him).[107]

In her scrapbook she even gives a description of where his house stood:

He lived in the street called formerly Apple-gate . . . Leading from St Nicholas Church to the West Bridge – the house is a very small one, and stands in the middle of the left hand side, as you go from the church.[108]

Whilst Susanna had sympathy with all of the dissenters, she had particular sympathy with Albert Cockshaw, who was the brother of one of her most intimate friends, Jeanette Cockshaw. He was one of Leicester's leading radical dissenters and a member of the Independent Chapel on Gallowtree Gate. For many years, prior to 1841, he had been active in many radical causes, including the anti-slavery movement and because of this he and Susanna may have had strong allegiances. In 1836, dissatisfied with the lack of radicalism in the Whig supporting newspaper, the *Leicester Chronicle*, Albert started a new weekly newspaper called the *Leicestershire Mercury*, of which he was the printer, the publisher and the editor. Whether, or not, it was the newspaper that placed a strain on his finances is unknown, but he was declared bankrupt in 1840 and was thus forced to sell the newspaper. So rather than Susanna being just concerned about the detrimental effects on the Church of England, she may also have been concerned for the wellbeing of her friend's brother, his wife, Ann, and their family, particularly if Albert faced a prison sentence, like William Baines. It could have meant financial catastrophe for the whole family, something Susanna herself had been familiar with in her own family.

At the time of Susanna's death, in 1842, her death certificate records her as living on King Street. St Mary de Castro parish register, however, records her residence, at the time of her death, to be Marquis Street. As Marquis Street runs off King Street it is possible that her house may have stood on the corner of both. King Street was laid out shortly after the building of the Crescent, at the bottom of King Street, circa 1810. Most of the housing consisted of large villas, but towards the end of Susanna's life factories and warehouses were beginning to creep in, making it a less desirable place to live. Before living on King Street, Susanna is known to have lived on London Road and before that she lived, for many years, on St Augustine Island, in Bromkinsthorpe, where her father and great grandfather had owned various pieces of land. Living very close by at that time was her close friend, Elizabeth Heyrick, who had lived at Bow Bridge House as a young married woman and as a widow.

There seems to be some confusion about the actual date of Susanna's death. On her gravestone she is recorded as dying on 11 February, 1842. A biographer also records her as dying at 10.30 am on 11 February. However, the date given on her death certificate is 4 February and this was registered on the 12 February. To confuse matters even further the *Leicester Journal* records her death as having taken place on 10 February. St Mary De Castro parish register records the funeral as having taken place on 15 February. It is, therefore, difficult to come to any firm conclusion about the date of death, although it was likely to have been 11 February as this is the date given on her gravestone. The cause of death is, perhaps, more certain. The certificate names the cause of death to be 'Decay of Nature' and this tends to confirm the information given in the brief biographical sketch of her life, which states that she had suffered two strokes, one in 1841 and the other on 8 January 1842, which affected her right side. After the first stroke Susanna was nursed back to health at the home of her friend, Eleanor Frewen Turner, in Cold Overton. However, at the time of her death it was a relative and not a friend who was present. It was Ann Woodford, nee Thornton, who was the wife of Susanna's cousin, John Woodford of Kibworth Harcourt.

Susanna was buried in the churchyard, near the north porch, of St Mary de Castro, where her simple gravestone can still be seen today. Simplicity in death seems to have been Susanna's preference and this is borne out in her chosen form of funeral procession:

> It is my very earnest desire that I may not be taken to my grave in the hearse with feathers, but in the plain little hearse.[109]

The chief family mourners at the funeral were William Mosley Watts, of Barnes, and his son of Exeter College. Other family mourners were Mrs and Miss Woodford and four other family members, who are not named. The

Woodfords are more than likely Ann, the wife of John Woodford, of Kibworth Harcourt, who was present at the time of Susanna's death, and her daughter, Elizabeth, who was named as a beneficiary in Susanna's will. Friends attending the funeral included: Eleanor Frewen Turner and her son, Charles Frewen, William Heyrick, the executor of her will, Mrs Macaulay (most probably Ann Macaulay, who was the widow of Aulay Macaulay) and Jeanette Cockshaw. According to the *Leicester Journal* there were also many of Leicester's elderly poor at Susanna's graveside.[110] The *Leicester Chronicle* is more dramatic in its description of the graveside scene '. . . in the churchyard crowds of aged poor brought their tears to embalm the memory of their great benefactor.'[111] Her charitable work amongst the elderly poor of the Town had obviously been much appreciated and remembered. The *Leicester Chronicle* is also keen to point out that it was not just the elderly who wished to pay their last respects '. . . numbers of youthful and independent eyes bore testimony to the estimation in which she was held.'[112] Shortly after her death the brief memoir of Susanna's life *Hymns and Poems of the Late Susanna Watts: with a few Recollections of her Life* was written anonymously and published and printed by J Waddington, Booksellers, of High Street. Samuel Coltman writes some years later that:

> . . . at her [Susanna's] death, memoirs of her life were not wanting to recall her beneficent actions, her poems too were published, at least selections from them, and all possible respect shown to her consistent with the known modesty of her character.[113]

Despite these accolades, Susanna believed herself to have failed in her literary career, claiming in a letter to Maria Edgeworth, that 'I have been an unsuccessful manufacturer of verse and translation.'[114] She may not have produced the great novels of Maria Edgeworth, like *Castle Rackrent,* but given the help, advice and encouragement that Maria clearly thought she needed, who knows what she might have achieved?

Susanna's will confirms her benevolent and caring nature so valued by many of her friends. Her gratitude and benevolence shown towards servants of the family is evidence of this. Her mother's servant, as previously mentioned, received acknowledgement for her dedicated service. Susanna's own faithful servant, Mary Brown, also received recognition for her loyalty. She was bequeathed a third of Susanna's furniture, from which she was allowed to select items of her own choosing, plus ten pounds in money, various articles of Susanna's clothing, three silver teaspoons, an old tablespoon and a bible. She also wished that Mary should 'have good mourning given to her'.[115] Susanna's benevolence extended beyond her family, friends and servants to other people who had touched upon her life. No one seems to have been forgotten in her will. Attached to it was a separate memorandum which listed a number of 'poor persons' who were to be given bequests out of the residue of her estate. Of these people Robert and Sarah Jones were marked with an asterisk as a couple that were to be 'particularly remembered'. Also written on the memorandum was the following sentiment:

> I humbly beg the Great Disposer to enable me to dispose of the little property I shall leave to those who shall most need it. That as far as I can I may remember the poor – having myself been poor, & having by the bounty of our heavenly father been supplied & fed.[116]

The people who had helped Susanna in her final days were also to be remembered:

> Let all those who have done me kind offices in the House in my sickness and death be remembered, perhaps in some articles of goods which may be useful to them.[117]

The separate memoranda attached to Susanna's will had not been officially drawn up by a solicitor, or signed by witnesses. Consequently, after her death two people, Emma Kirby and Eliza Bankart, who had known Susanna up until her death, but were not beneficiaries in the will, were called upon to swear, on oath, that they were written, to the best of their knowledge, in the 'proper' handwriting of Susanna.

Susanna's charitable bequests were rather limited. The only beneficiary specifically named was Thurmaston Sunday School, which had made frequent donations to the Leicester Ladies Anti-Slavery Society. Any other donations to charitable causes were left to the discretion of her executor, William Heyrick.

The final tribute paid to Susanna in the *Leicester Chronicle's* obituary was the printing of one of her poems, entitled *The True Gem*. In many ways it is a fitting end to her life which was obviously lived out according to her Christian beliefs:

> There is a gem of peerless worth,
> A treasure of the mind;
> Search all the mines of all the earth,
> No prize so rich you'll find.

It is not Genius - that may blaze,
A diamond dazzling bright;
Which sparkling keen with shifting rays
Emits no useful light.

It is not Wit, whose rosy beams
Like glowing rushes dart;
It is not Learnings golden streams
No Science, Taste, or Art.

It is a gem of peerless worth,
It holds the place of wealth;
It brings the light of heav'n to earth;
And sickness turns to health.

It is the poor and contrite heart,
Whose value, who may tell?
For there the High and Holy One,
Himself shall deign to dwell.

Thou dread Supreme! – all other gifts
Withhold – but oh! Impart
The richest boon that thou canst give-
A poor and contrite heart.[118]

Conclusion

When writing a biography, no matter how small, you really begin to feel that you know the person whose life you have poked about in. Writing about Susanna has been no exception. It is no easy task to piece together someone's whole life, indeed I think it is an impossibility, particularly when the sources are few. I have merely gathered together fragments of information from all manner of sources and in so doing I have sometimes felt akin to Mary Shelley's Victor Frankenstein. Some of the trails followed have run cold, but others have yielded valuable information, the identity of Susanna's mother being a case in point.

The most invaluable source of biographical information I have used has, undoubtedly, been Susanna's own scrapbook. She was obviously well aware of its historical and biographical value to future generations and this is why she gave it to her life-long friend, Mary Ann Coltman, for safe-keeping. The other women who became its custodians were equally aware of its intrinsic value and importance to our understanding of an exceptional woman's life in eighteenth and nineteenth century Leicester. Not only did Susanna wish to bequeath her scrapbook to us, but I also believe she wished us to know what she looked like and this is why there is a self-portrait pasted into the scrapbook.

Susanna was clearly a very well liked and respected woman in the town. Her biographers, friends and the newspapers all testify to this. She was a strong minded woman, who had a passionate, caring and principled nature. Unlike many women of her time, Susanna did not allow herself to become ensnared by the female conventions and restrictions of the day. She tended rather to follow her own path. Being a talented and intellectual woman enabled her to make friends with similarly gifted people in the town. She seems to have been a loyal friend, who understood the true meaning of friendship and all of the pleasures and benefits it brings to one's life. Her friends played an important role in her life, by sharing similar opinions and beliefs. They were also supportive of her in times of need. Her life-long friendship with Elizabeth Heyrick and her sister, Mary Ann Coltman, was particularly significant in a variety of ways, not least in the fact that they were more like sisters than friends and, indeed, called each other so.

The close female friendships that Susanna had were particularly important regarding her intellectual development and emotional support. For during their lifetime women were formally excluded from participating in all of the major institutions of society and this meant they had few other resources, than themselves, with which to develop their intellectual skills. Women known as Bluestockings had been cultivating intellectual openings for women throughout the eighteenth century and although their aims and activities have largely been considered to be conservative, they nevertheless challenged male dominance by their very existence. They also defied the norm that women were intellectually incompetent and through their friendship circles they provided an all female artistic, literary and intellectual alternative.

Susanna and her friends were very much a part of this Bluestocking tradition, although they came at the tail end of the major period of activity. Nevertheless, it can be seen in their poetic response to the Reverend Robert Throsby that they very much identified with the Bluestocking label, despite it being an abusive term by this time. They used Throsby's derogatory name calling of 'a set of dragons' to their own advantage:

> A Dragon is by Naturalist's defined,
> A wondrous creature of the <u>Serpent </u>kind;
> And serpents – Holy Writ this truth supplies,
> Are ever deemed an emblem of <u>the Wise;</u> [1]

Here they combine the mythology of the dragon with the pre-Christian power of the serpent. In most early cultures the serpent was one of the Goddess's most potent and powerful symbols of wisdom, immortality and totality. Being a united and intimate all female friendship group they clearly felt able to withstand Throsby's mockery.

The female friendship group of Susanna, Elizabeth Heyrick and Mary Ann Coltman, continued to develop and gain strength over the years. In 1824, with the publication of their anti-slavery periodical, *The Humming Bird,* they had become even more powerfully cemented together and, perhaps, even more conscious about the role of women in society. This is borne out in an article they wrote for *The Humming Bird,* during 1825. Here they are clearly intent on writing what was essentially a wake-up call to women:

> The time is gone by when the energies of the female sex were wasted upon laborious and everlasting tasks of needle-work, and their literature was confined to cookery books. [2]

We have seen that Susanna had spent many hours, when younger, designing needlework pictures and works of art created from hair and feathers. These so called accomplishments, had, like her writing, brought its rewards and accolades. Had she now, as the quotation above indicates, abandoned these pursuits and seen them as only trivial activities? The labelling of traditional feminine arts as accomplishments was, to all intents and purposes, a derogatory term used to distinguish them from more prestigious male pursuits. However, it also has to be said that much of the art work done by girls and women, particularly that of samplers, although often very beautiful and decorative, was nevertheless tedious, time consuming and controlling work.

In the first editorial of the Humming Bird, the three women describe themselves as a 'triple union' and 'an ancient Sisterhood' born 'Anno Mundi, one'.[3] In other words they saw their friendship to be as old, all but one year, as the creation of the world, itself. So strong was this sisterly bonding that they felt 'no man may put us asunder, or, by any power or art whatsoever, interrupt our triple union . . .'[4] This 'triple union' is then likened by them to the strength and power of other triple female unions in Greek and Roman mythology. For they next write '. . . but whether we are *Fates, Furies,* or *Graces,* you shall know presently.'[5] The Fates were the three daughters, Clotho, Lachesis and Atropos, of Zeus and the Goddess of Justice, Themis. They were ever prevailing and had the power to decide man's destiny and laughed at his feeble attempts to cheat them. The Furies were the three daughters, Megaera, Tisiphone and Alecto, of Mother Earth and the blood of the castrated Uranus. They were powerful divinities that personified conscience and when called upon to act they hounded their victims until they died in a 'furor' of madness or torment. The Graces were the three daughters, Aglaia, Euphrosyne and Thalia, of Zeus and the nymph, Eurgnome. They brought joy, charm and beauty and presided over banquets and dances, bringing to them happiness and goodwill for both gods and mortals.

In a society where they knew their place, as women, to be ' . . . the inferior labourers of the vineyard',[6] Susanna, Elizabeth and Mary Ann refused to be intimidated, or challenged by male authority and realised that the only way they had strength was through unity. Although all three were religious women, Susanna being a member of the Church of England, Elizabeth a Quaker and Mary Ann, a Christian, but with no real affiliation to any denomination, they, like many women throughout history, seemed to be looking to the ancient religions and mythology of the Greeks and Romans for female empowerment.

Their united power was one of their main strengths when fighting the abolitionist cause and this is why women had joined together to form the Female Society for the Relief of the British Negro Slaves. Secure in their unity, they became increasingly involved in a whole range of pressure group activities which developed their skills, increased their confidence and gave them a collective sense of identity. They argued for an end to the slave trade on moral grounds and natural rights, but also on religious grounds. This was made very evident in an article which appeared in *The Humming Bird:*

> It must be repeated that the question is a Religious one. We have already proved, and the argument is so important that it ought to be frequently reiterated, that it was *solely* by the influence of Christianity on the minds and consciences of men, that Slavery in England was abolished, and this even in Catholic times. Men freed their slaves *for the love of God;* for the *safety of their own souls.* The same principle must, in the nature of things, effect the abolition of African Slavery. There is no other engine mighty enough to remove this long-rooted crime from this earth . . .There is no middle way. Slavery and Christianity cannot exist in the same nation.[7]

Susanna and her friends were, then, at the very forefront, moving beyond a supportive role by setting up their female only abolitionist groups and societies.

Female friendship circles, such as Susanna's, are central to our understanding of feminist development in the late eighteenth and early nineteenth centuries, although there is still much research to be done in the provinces if we are to get a broader and more accurate picture. The lack of information available about Susanna and her friends, particularly the lost records of the Leicester Women's Anti-Slavery Society, has been a very frustrating part of the research, not least because it serves to cut us off from knowing who the women were that joined, how they thought and the actions they took. However, the information that has randomly survived has shown Susanna and her friends to have been a force to be reckoned with. They broke down the conventional barriers and acted in public. They refused to be intimidated and challenged male authority. One wonders what they might have gone on to achieve had they lived longer and been young enough, for the first organized movement for women's rights was borne out of the anti-slavery movement. Matters concerning women's public role came to a head in London in 1840, when women delegates from both Britain and American were barred from taking part, at the World Anti-Slavery Convention. Would Susanna and her friends have again been prepared, like they had in 1825, to "bear the burden and heat of the day"? [8]

Susanna's writings and translations were undoubtedly a means to earn a living, but I also suspect that it was more than this in that she wrote passionately about subjects dear to her own heart, like the welfare of animals, in the hope that her writings would educate others to think and act in a like-minded way. Her poetry was her most powerful written form of expression and from the evidence that survives it certainly seems to have been her favourite chosen route for documenting her beliefs, opinions and sentiments. Poetry was, and still is, a very powerful social and political tool and Susanna was very adept at using it to this end.

Writing for a public audience was the only real means for women to achieve a voice, for society deemed it unacceptable behaviour for a woman to speak at a public meeting. Even by writing, Susanna ran the risk of public condemnation and this is why many women either used a male pseudonym, or remained anonymous, when publishing a book. Her book *The Animal's Friend* was clearly written with a great passion to educate and dissuade others from using acts of cruelty to animals. To put her name to such a publication, in which her argument was so forcefully put, was indeed a brave act. On the opening page she makes no attempt, like many other women writers of her time, to apologise for her audacity and presumption in stating such forthright opinions. In asserting her identity in this way Susanna can be seen as unrepresentative of her sex, at that time.

When daring to use her own name on one publication it is interesting to speculate why she chose to remain the anonymous writer of A *Walk Through Leicester.* Did she believe that people would be less inclined to buy a copy if it were known that it had been written by a woman? It would also be of interest to know if she had remained anonymous, or used a male pseudonym for any other publications, including her four volume novel. The novel, had it survived, would, like many other first novels, possibly have been semi-autobiographical and this would have given greater insight into Susanna's life and consciousness.

Considering the fact that Susanna was a woman living in an age when it was extremely difficult for middle class women to earn any sort of living, she did remarkably well to achieve even the moderate success and accolades that she did. Added to the problem of her being a single woman was the fact that she lived in a small provincial town and experienced severe familial problems that left her in financial penury from a young age. Susanna's main writing success has to be her nineteenth century guide to Leicester. Having written such an early guide certainly puts Susanna at the very forefront of this genre. She clearly had a great love for her native town and county, as shown in her poem, *Old Leicestershire*, and, consequently, wanted visitors to enjoy it, too.

Susanna was not just content to write about social and political issues she also invested a good deal of her time and energy in becoming actively involved with a whole variety of causes. In the days before the Welfare State and Old Age Pensions she cared for the elderly of the Town for over two decades. Not only was she a friend to the elderly, helping to relieve their poverty and hardship, but she also cared passionately about the sufferings of others. Her own mother was a case in point, as were the people in the south and west of Ireland. But above all, it was the plight of the African slave that Susanna fought long and hard to relieve.

When I began writing this biography I was most excited by the prospect of it, but I was also conscious that there were very few records from which to build any kind of real picture of Susanna. Like most people when doing research I have been frustrated, disappointed, excited, surprised, puzzled, impatient, exhausted and elated. I have looked at what records were available, asked many questions, interpreted what I have found and written a biography that is longer than I first intended. Had someone else looked at the same material then they might well have interpreted it in a different way and written something entirely different.

References

Introduction

1. Susanna Watts, *A Walk Through Leicester; being A Guide To Strangers, containing A Description of the Town And Its Environs, with remarks upon its History and Antiquities* (Leicester University Press, 1967) p.vii.

2. Susanna Watts, *Scrapbook* (The Record Office of Leicester, Leicestershire and Rutland, Rare Books, L.A. Watts) p.455.

Susanna Watts – A Life

1. Samuel Coltman, *Times Stepping Stones or Memorials of Four Generations of a Family by a Member of the Same* (The Record Office of Leicester, Leicestershire and Rutland, 15D57/387) p.7.

2. Susanna Watts, *Scrapbook* (letter from Maria Edgeworth to Mary Sneyd, 12 September 1802) pp.91- 94.

3. John Nichols, *The History and Antiquities of the County of Leicester,* Volume 4, Part 2 (Printed by Nichols and Son, London) p.570.

4. Ernest B. Frizelle & Janet D. Martin, *The Leicester Royal Infirmary 1771 to 1971* (Leicester No.1 Hospital Management Committee, 1971) p.17.

5. The will of John Watts (The Record Office of Leicester, Leicestershire and Rutland, PR/T/1770/205).

6. Ibid.

7. Ibid.

8. St Mary De Castro, Leicester, Parish Registers (The Record Office of Leicester, Leicestershire and Rutland, DE/683).

9. Anonymous, *Hymns and Poems of the Late Susanna Watts with a few Recollections of her Life* (Printed and Published by J Waddington, Booksellers, Leicester, 1842) p.55.

10. St Mary De Castro. op.cit.

11. Catherine Beale (edit), *Catherine Hutton and her Friends* (Cornish Brothers, Birmingham, 1895) p.161.

12. The will of John Watts. op.cit.

13. *Leicester Chronicle.* 19 February 1842. p.3.

14. *Leicester Journal.* 22 May 1807. p.3.

15. Samuel Coltman. op.cit. p.7.

16. Ibid. p.8.

17. The Death Certificate of Susanna Watts.

18. The will of Susanna Watts, 4 May 1826 (The Record Office of Leicester and Leicestershire and Rutland, PR/T/1843/153/1-3).

19. St Wilfreds, Kibworth Beauchamp, Parish Registers (The Record Office of Leicester, Leicestershire and Rutland, DE 5417).

20. Susanna Watts, *Scrapbook* (Letter from Maria Edgeworth to Mary Sneyd, 12 September 1802) pp.91- 94.

21. Anonymous, *Hymns and Poems of the Late Susanna Watts*. op.cit. p.57.

22. Ibid.

23. The will of Susanna Watts. op.cit. (Codicil E).

24. Charles James Billson, *Leicester Memoirs* (Edgar Backus, Leicester, 1924) p.67.

25. *Leicester Chronicle*. 19 February 1842. p.3.

26. John Nichols. op.cit. p.570.

27. Susanna Watts, *Scrapbook*. op.cit. p.367.

28. Anonymous, *Hymns and Poems of the Late Susanna Watts*. op.cit. p.57.

29. Samuel Coltman. op.cit. p.8.

30. *Leicester Chronicle*. 19 February 1842. p.3.

31. Clara Parkes (foreword), in Susanna Watts, *Scrapbook* (The Record Office of Leicester, Leicestershire and Rutland, Rare Books, LA Watts*)* p.367.

32. Susanna Watts, *Scrapbook* (Letter from Maria Edgeworth to Mary Sneyd, 12 September 1802) pp.91- 94.

33. Cheryl Turner, *Living by the Pen: Women Writers in the Eighteenth Century* (Routledge, 1994) p.113.

34. Susanna Watts, *Scrapbook* (Letter from Maria Edgeworth to Mary Sneyd, 12 September 1802) pp.91-94.

35. Dale Spender, *Mothers of the Novel: 100 good women writers before Jane Austin* (Pandora, London, 1986) p.287.

36. Ibid.

37. Marilyn Butler, *Maria Edgeworth,* in Janet Todd (ed), *A Dictionary of British and American Women Writers 1600-1800* (Methuen, London) p.111.

38. Anonymous, *Hymns and Poems of the Late Susanna Watts*. op.cit. p.55.

39. Ibid. p.57.

40. Susanna Watts, *Scrapbook* (Letter from Maria Edgeworth to Mary Sneyd, 12 September 1802) pp.91-94.

41. Clara Parkes. op.cit.

42. John Heyrick (junior), *First Flights* (Privately published, posthumously, in Leicester, 18 August 1797) p.12.

43. Anonymous, *Hymns and Poems of the Late Susanna Watts*. op.cit. p.57.

44. Catherine Beale (edit). op.cit. pp.159-60.

45. *Leicester Chronicle*. 19 February 1842. p.3.

46. Susanna Watts, *A Walk Through Leicester*. op.cit. p.5.

47. Ibid. p.25.

48. William Gardiner, *Music and Friends or Pleasant Recollections of A Dilettante* (Volumes 1 and 2, Longman, London and Coombe and Crossley, Leicester, 1838) p.106.

49. Susanna Watts, *Scrapbook*. op.cit. p.280.

50. Catherine Beale (edit). op.cit. p.223.

51. Susanna Watts, *Scrapbook* (Letter from Maria Edgeworth to Mary Sneyd, 12 September 1802) pp.91-94.

52. Ibid.

53. The will of Susanna Watts. op.cit. (Codicil B).

54. Susanna Watts, *The Animal's Friend: A Collection of Observations and Facts Tending to Restrain Cruelty and to Inculcate Kindness Towards Animals* (Simpkin and Marshall) p.93.

55. Ibid. p.4.

56. Ibid.

57. Ibid. p.16.

58. Ibid. p.1.

59. Susanna Watts, *The Insects Council* (printed by J. Hatchard & Son, Hurst, Chance and Co, Simpkin and Marshall and Cockshaws, Leicester, 1828), Introduction.

60. Samuel Coltman. op.cit. p.7.

61. Catherine Beale (edit), op.cit. p.147.

62. Samuel Coltman. op.cit. p.1.

63. Ibid. p.7.

64. Susanna Watts, *Scrapbook*. op.cit. p.545.

65. Ibid.

66. Susanna Watts, *A Walk Through Leicester*. op.cit. pp.1-3.

67. Susanna Watts, *Scrapbook*. op.cit. p.504.

68. The will of Susanna Watts. op.cit. (4 May 1826).

69. Clara Parkes, op.cit.

70. Susanna Watts, *Scrapbook.* op.cit. p.320.

71. Catherine Beale (edit). op.cit. p.162.

72. *Leicester Journal.* 18 October 1822. p.3.

73. Ibid. 22 November 1822. p.3.

74. Susanna Watts, *Scrapbook* (Letter to Maria Edgeworth, 10 March 1830) p.391.

75. Ibid. p.547.

76. Clare Midgley, *Women Against Slavery: The British Campaigns 1780-1870* (Routledge, 1992) p.76.

77. *The Humming Bird or Morsels of Information on the Subject of Slavery with Various Miscellaneous Articles.* volume 1, number 7, June 1825 (A. Cockshaw, Leicester, 1825-26) p.201.

78. Ibid. p.196.

79. Ibid. (volume 1, number 8, July 1825) p.246.

80. Ibid. (volume 1, number 1, December 1824) p.3.

81. Ibid. (volume 1, number 2, January 1825) p.58.

82. Ibid. (volume 1, number 1, December 1824) p.5.

83. Ibid. (volume 1, number 1, December 1824 and volume 1, number 10, September 1825)p.3 and p.314.

84. Ibid. (volume 1, number 3, February 1825) p.84.

85. Ibid. (volume 1, number 1, preface) p.3.

86. Ibid. (volume 1, number 7, June 1825) p.192.

87. First Report of the Female Society for the Relief of British Negro Slaves 1825 to 1826 (Birmingham City Archives, Central Library, Microfilm M2/IIR 62) p.3.

88. Ibid. (Report for 1827/8) p.37.

89. Ibid.

90. The 1828 Reports of the Birmingham and Calne Female Society for the Relief of British Negro Slaves (Birmingham City Archives, Central Library, Microfilm M2/IIR 62).

91. Kenneth Corfield, *Elizabeth Heyrick: Radical Quaker,* in Gail Malmgreen (edit) *Religion in the Lives of English Women 1760-1830* (Croom Helm, 1986) p.50.

92. Susanna Watts, *Scrapbook.* op.cit. p.303.

93. Catherine Beale (edit). op.cit. p.224.

94. Susanna Watts, *Scrapbook.* op.cit. p.313.

95. Ibid. p.309.

96. Ibid.

97. Anonymous, *Hymns and Poems of the Late Susanna Watts.* op.cit. p.63.

98.   Clara Parkes. op.cit.

99.   Susanna Watts, *Scrapbook*. op.cit. p.486.

100. Ibid. pp.475-479.

101. *Leicester Chronicle*. 19 February 1842. p.3.

102. Catherine Beale (edit). op.cit. p.161.

103. Susanna Watts, *Scrapbook*. op.cit. p.480.

104. *Leicestershire Mercury*. 22 May 1841. p.3.

105. Jack Simmons, *Leicester: The Ancient Borough to 1860* (Alan Sutton, 1983) p.168.

106. Florence E. Skillington, *The Plain Man's History of Leicester* (Edgar Backus, Leicester, 1950) p.102.

107. Susanna Watts, *Scrapbook*. op.cit. p.348.

108. Ibid.

109. The will of Susanna Watts. op.cit. (Codicil D).

110. *Leicester Journal*. 18 February 1842. p.3.

111. *Leicester Chronicle*. 19 February 1842. p.3.

112. Ibid.

113. Samuel Coltman. op.cit. p.9.

114. Susanna Watts, *Scrapbook* (Letter to Maria Edgeworth, 10 March 1830) p.391.

115. The will of Susanna Watts. op.cit. (4 May 1826).

116. Ibid. (Codicil C).

117. Ibid.

118. *Leicester Chronicle*. 19 February 1842. p.3.

Conclusion

1.   Susanna Watts, *Scrapbook*. op.cit. p.545.

2.   *The Humming Bird* (volume 1, number 7, June 1825) p.195.

3.   Ibid. (volume 1, number 1, December 1824) p.3.

4.   Ibid.

5.   Ibid.

6.   Ibid. (volume 1, number 6, May 1825) p.193.

7.   Ibid.

8.   Ibid. (volume 1, number 7, June 1825) p.195.

Bibliography

Anonymously, *The Hummingbird or Morsels of Information on the Subject of Slavery with Various Miscellaneous Articles* (printed and published by A Cockshaw, Leicester 1825).

Anonymously, *Hymns and Poems of the late Susanna Watts: with a few Recollections of her Life* (Printed by J Waddington Booksellers, Leicester, 1842).

Catherine Beale (edit), *Catherine Hutton and her Friends* (Cornish Brothers, Birmingham, 1895).

J.D. Bennett, *Susanna Watts – Author of Leicester's First Guidebook* (personal notes for BBC Radio Leicester programmes).

Charles James Billson, *Leicester Memoirs* (Edgar Backus, Leicester, 1924).

Barbara Caine, *English Feminism 1780-1980* (Oxford University Press, 1997).

Samuel Coltman, *Times Stepping Stones or Memorials of Four Generations of a Family - by a Member of the Same* (The Record Office of Leicester, Leicestershire and Rutland, 15D/57/450).

Kenneth Corfield, *Elizabeth Heyrick: Radical Quaker,* in Gail Malmgreen (edit), *Religion in the Lives of English Women 1760-1830* (Croom Helm, 1986).

Colin Ellis, *History in Leicester 55 BC—AD 1976* (Information Bureau, Recreational Services Department, Leicester City Council, 1976).

Ernest B. Frizelle and Janet D. Martin, *The Leicester Royal Infirmary 1771-1971* (Leicester Number 1 Hospital Management Committee, 1971).

Ernest B. Frizelle, *The Life and Times of the Royal Infirmary: The Making of a Teaching Hospital 1766-1980* (The Leicester Medical Society, The Post Graduate Medical Centre and the Royal Infirmary, Leicester, 1988).

William Gardiner, *Music and Friends or Pleasant Recollections of A Dilettante.* Volumes 1 and 2 (Longman, London and Coombe and Crossley, Leicester, 1838).

Elizabeth Heyrick, *Immediate not gradual Abolition, or an inquiry into the shortest, safest and most effectual means of getting rid of West Indian Slavery* (Knight and Bugster, London, 1824).

John Heyrick (junior), *First Flights* (Published privately, posthumously, 1797).

Agnes Fielding Johnson, *Glimpses of Ancient Leicester in Six Periods* (Clarke and Satchell, Leicester and Simpkin, Marshall, Hamilton, Kent and Co, Limited, 1906).

Sidney Lee, *Dictionary of National Biography* (Smith ,Elder & Co, 1899).

Leicester Journal.

Leicester Chronicle.

Leicestershire Mercury.

Clare Midgley, *Women Against Slavery: The British Campaigns 1780-1870* (Routledge, 1992).

John Nichols, *The History and Antiquities of the County of Leicester*. Volume 1 and 4, Part 2 (Printed by and for John Nichols & Son, London, 1811).

A. Temple Patterson, *Radical Leicester: A History of Leicester 1780-1850* (Leicester University Press, 1975).

Jack Simmons, *Leicester: The Ancient Borough to 1860* (Alan Sutton, 1983).

Florence E. Skillington, *The Coltman's of the Newarke at Leicester* (W. Thornley and Son, 1934).

Florence E. Skillington, *The Plain Man's History of Leicester* (Edgar Backus, Leicester, 1950).

Dale Spender, *Women of Ideas: And What Men Have Done To Them* (Ark Paperbacks, 1983).

Dale Spender, *Mothers of The Novel: 100 good women writers before Jane Austen* (Pandora, 1986).

The Coltman Family Papers and Letters (The Record Office of Leicester, Leicestershire and Rutland, 15/D/57).

The Female Society for the Relief of British Negro Slaves 1825 to 1919 (Birmingham City Archives, Central Library, Microfilm M2/11R 62).

The Heyrick Family Papers and Letters 1749 to 1865 (The Record Office of Leicester, Leicestershire and Rutland, 109.30/34).

The Parish Registers of St Mary de Castro, Leicester (The Record Office of Leicester, Leicestershire and Rutland, DE/683).

The Parish Registers of St Martins, Leicester (The Record Office of Leicester, Leicestershire and Rutland, DE 1564).

The Parish Registers of St Wilfreds, Kibworth Beauchamp, Leicestershire (The Record Office of Leicester, Leicestershire and Rutland, DE 5417).

The will of William Heyrick (Public Record Office PROB 11/2234).

The will of John Watts (senior) (The Record Office of Leicester, Leicestershire and Rutland).

The will of John Watts (The Record Office of Leicester, Leicestershire and Rutland, PR/T/1770/205).

The will of Susanna Watts (The Record Office of Leicester, Leicestershire and Rutland, PR/T/1843/153/1-3).

John Throsby, *The History and Antiquities of the Ancient Town of Leicester* (J. Brown, Leicester, 1791).

Cheryl Turner, *Living by the Pen: Women Writers in the Eighteenth Century* (Routledge, 1994).

Susanna Watts, *The Animals Friend: A Collection of Observations & Facts Tending to Restrain Cruelty & to Inculcate Kindness Towards Animals* (Simpkin and Marshall and C. Tilt, Circa 1830).

Susanna Watts, *Chinese Maxims: Translated from the Economy of Human Life into Heroic Verse* (printed in Leicester by John Gregory, 1784).

Susanna Watts, *Original Poems and Translations, particularly AMBRA from Lorenzo De Medici* (printed by Nichols and Son, London, 1802).

Susanna Watts, *The Insects Council* (printed by J. Hatchnard & Son, Hurst, Chance and Co, Simpkin and Marshall and Cockshaws, Leicester, 1828).

Susanna Watts, *The Wonderful Travels of Prince Fan-Feredin in the Country of Arcadia* (Northampton, printed by T. Dicey and Co for T & J Evans Paternoster Row, London, 1794).

Susanna Watts, *Scrapbook* (The Record Office of Leicester, Leicestershire and Rutland, Rare Books L.A. Watts).

Susanna Watts, *A Walk through Leicester: being A Guide To Strangers: containing A Description of the Town And Its Environs, with remarks upon its History And Antiquities* (Printed by T. Coombe, Leicester, 1804).

Susanna Watts, *A Walk through Leicester: being A Guide To Strangers: containing A Description of the Town And Its Environs, with remarks upon its History And Antiquities* (Printed by T. Coombe, Leicester, 1820).

Susanna Watts, *A Walk through Leicester: being A Guide To Strangers: containing A Description of the Town And Its Environs, with Remarks upon its History And Antiquities* (Printed by Thornley and Waddington, Leicester, 1902).

Susanna Watts, *A Walk through Leicester: being A Guide To Strangers: containing A Description of the Town And Its Environs, with remarks upon its History And Antiquities* (Leicester University Press, 1967).

William White, *History, Gazetteer and Directory of Leicester -1846.*